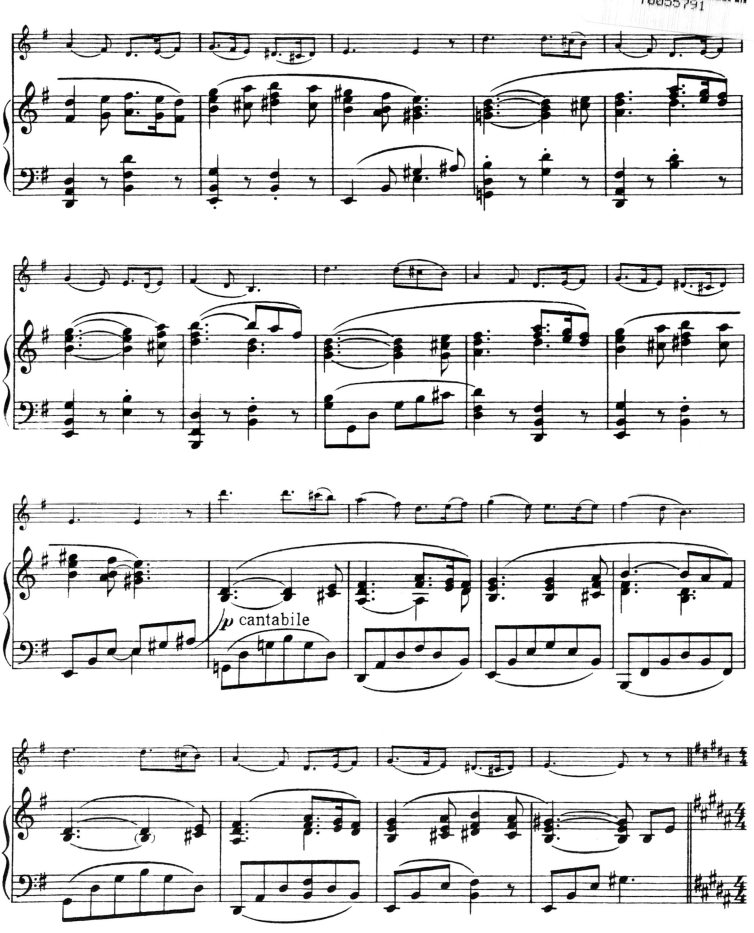

3

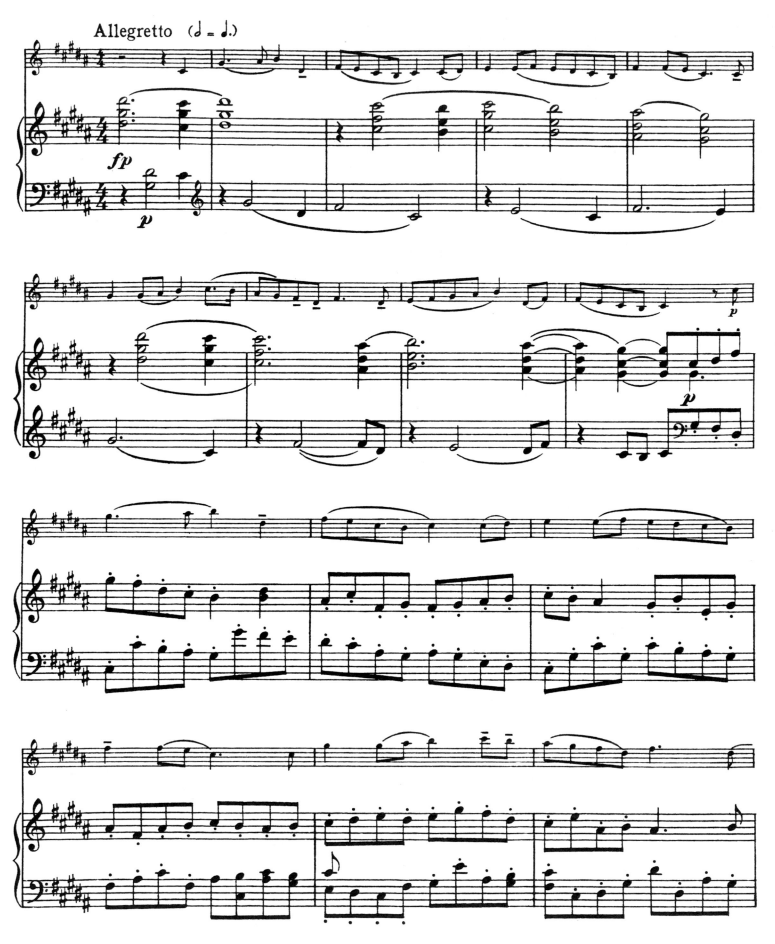

Allegretto (♩ = ♩.)

4

VIOLIN

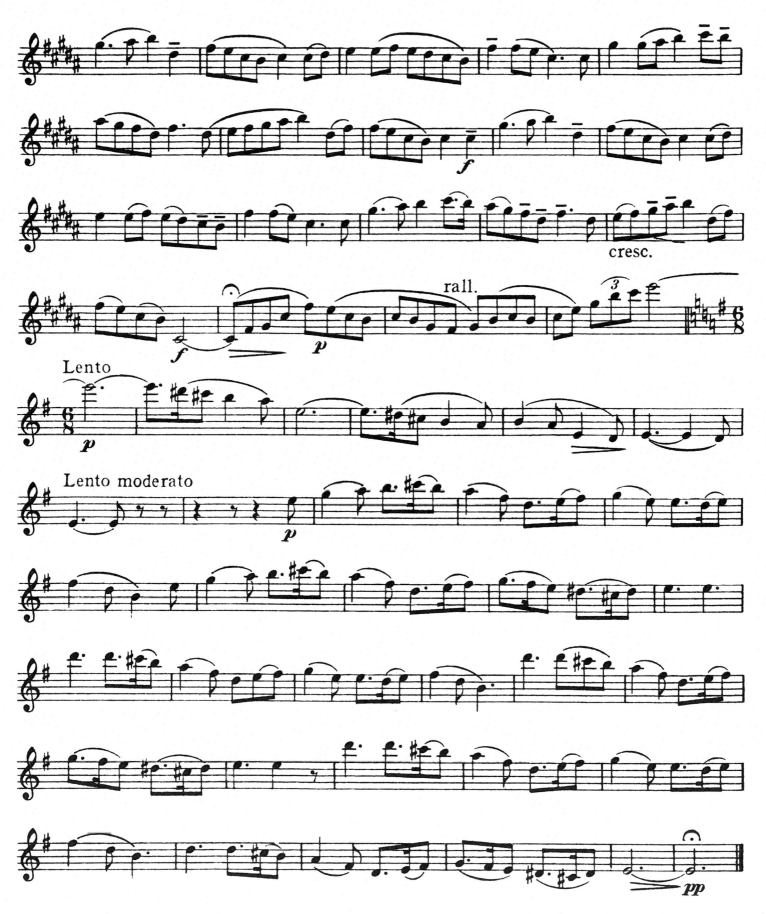

3

FANTASIA ON
GREENSLEEVES

Arranged for Violin and Pianoforte by
MICHAEL MULLINAR

R. VAUGHAN WILLIAMS

VIOLIN

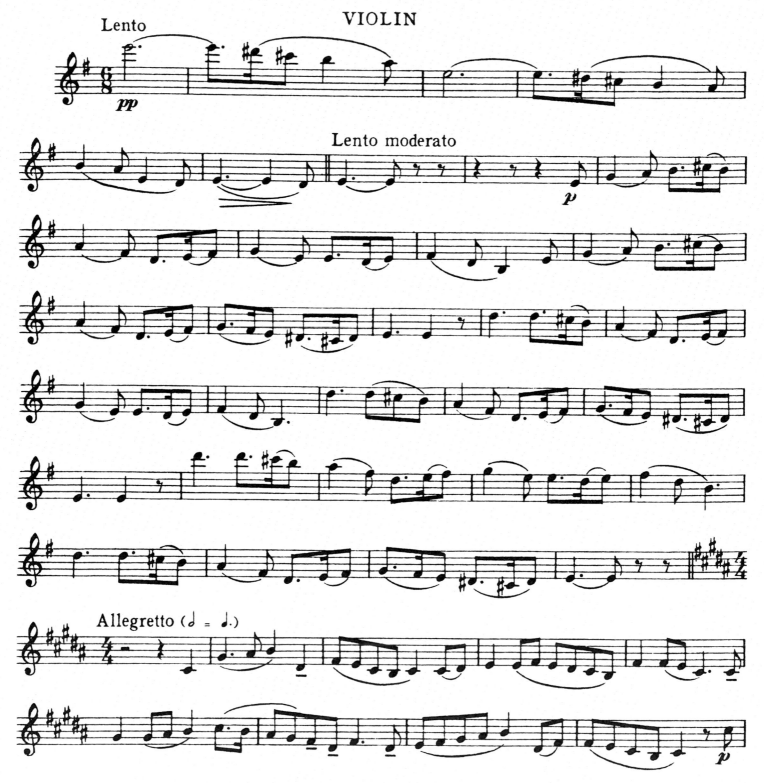

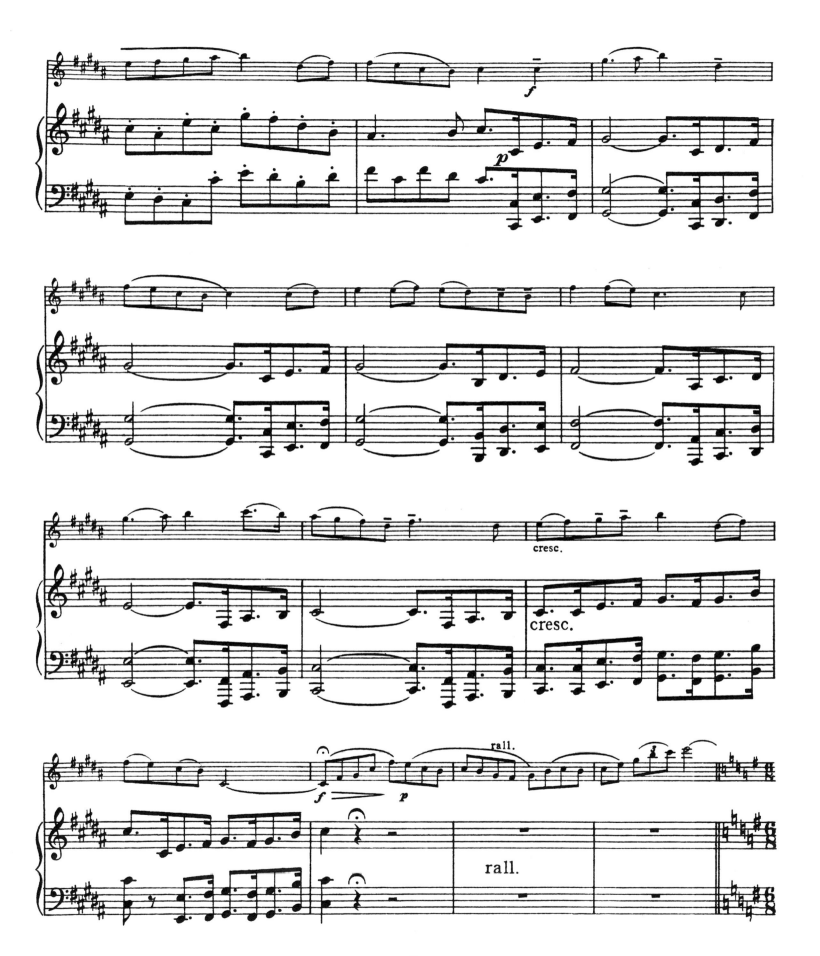

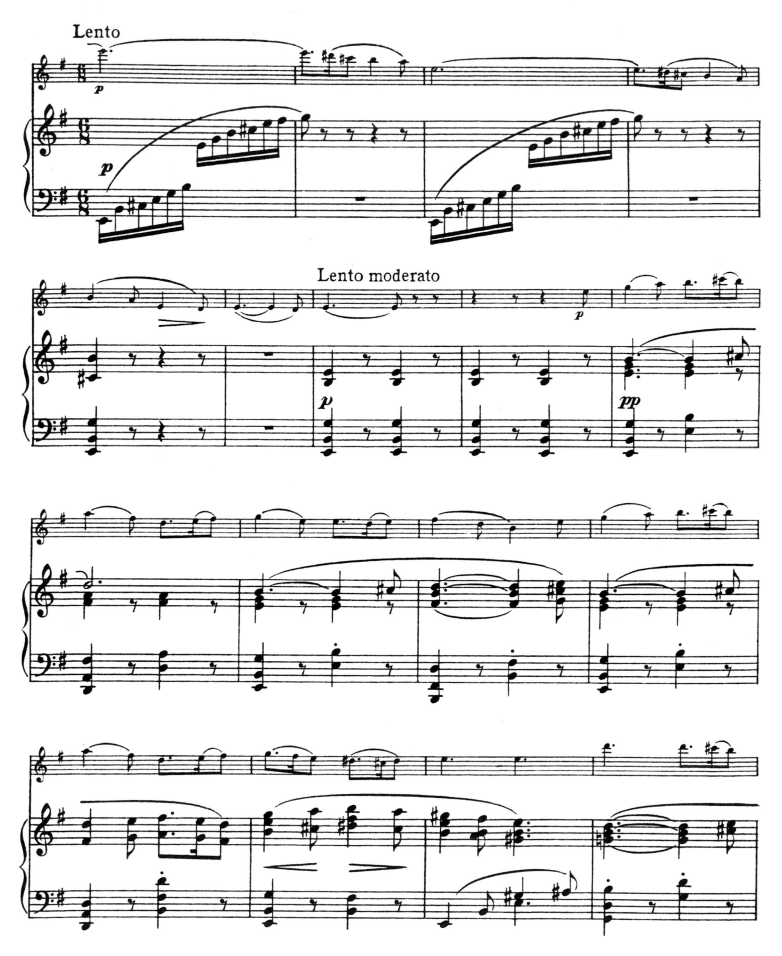

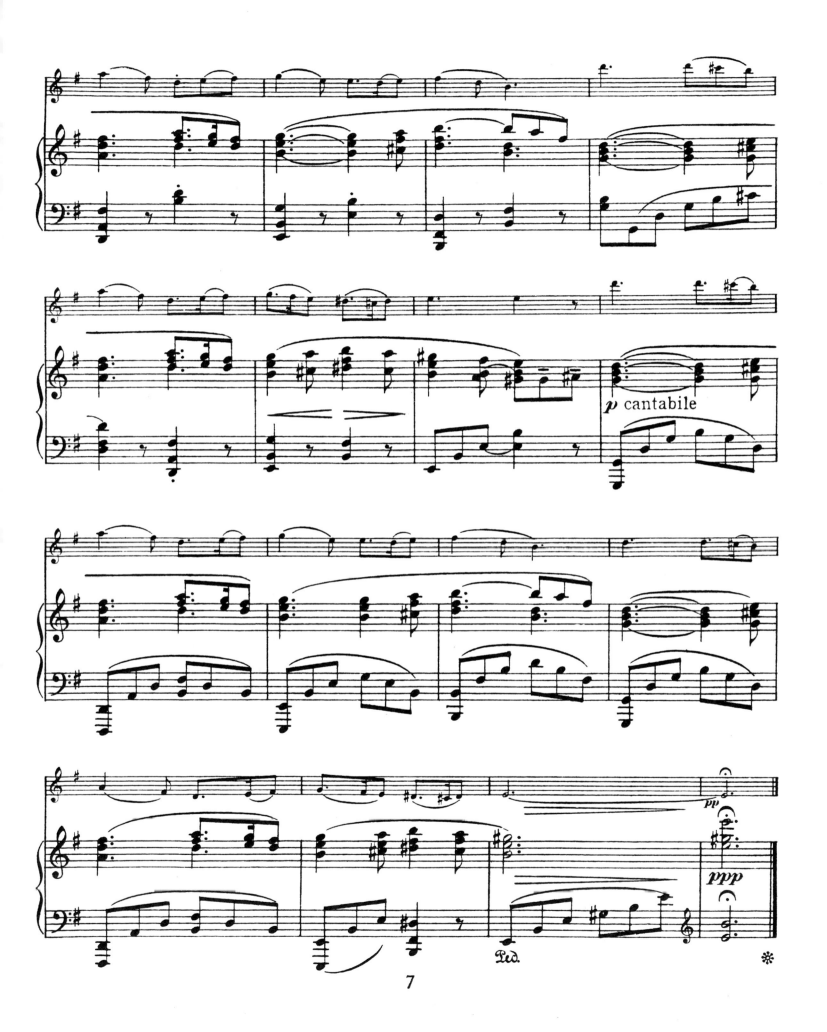

OXFORD
UNIVERSITY PRESS

ISBN 978-0-19-359307-7

9 780193 593077